PIANO VOCAL GUITAR

Billy Joel /

Additional editing and transcription
by David Rosenthal

ISBN 978-1-4584-1531-8

HAL•LEONARD® CORPORATION
7777 W. BLUEMOUND RD. P.O. BOX 13819 MILWAUKEE, WI 53213

In Australia Contact:
Hal Leonard Australia Pty. Ltd.
4 Lentara Court
Cheltenham, Victoria, 3192 Australia
Email: ausadmin@halleonard.com.au

For all works contained herein:
Unauthorized copying, arranging, adapting, recording, Internet posting, public performance,
or other distribution of the printed music in this publication is an infringement of copyright.
Infringers are liable under the law.

Visit Hal Leonard Online at
www.halleonard.com

CONTENTS

- 6   TRAVELIN' PRAYER
- 14   PIANO MAN
- 27   AIN'T NO CRIME
- 33   YOU'RE MY HOME
- 41   THE BALLAD OF BILLY THE KID
- 54   WORSE COMES TO WORST
- 59   STOP IN NEVADA
- 65   IF I ONLY HAD THE WORDS (TO TELL YOU)
- 70   SOMEWHERE ALONG THE LINE
- 78   CAPTAIN JACK

FORWORD

Having played keyboards in Billy Joel's band since 1993, I have become very familiar with his music. In 2008, Billy asked that I review the sheet music to his entire catalog of songs. As I am also a pianist, he entrusted me with the task of correcting or re-transcribing each piece as required, to ensure that the printed music represent his songs exactly as they were recorded.

The challenge was to find musical ways to combine Billy's piano parts and vocal melodies into a playable piano arrangement. First, the signature piano parts were transcribed and notated exactly as Billy played them on the original album (i.e. the classic intro to Piano Man, the honky tonk piano intro to Ain't No Crime, the piano flourishes in the verses of Captain Jack, etc., etc.). The vocal melodies were then incorporated into the piano part in a manner which preserves the original character of the song.

On songs like "You're My Home", where the main instrument is acoustic guitar, the arrangement is adapted to be playable on piano but still maintains the integrity of what was originally recorded. On "The Ballad of Billy The Kid", the piano part has been arranged to combine Billy's piano and vocal melodies along with the band and orchestral parts, while still including exactly what Billy plays in the piano solo sections.

All of the songs in this collection received the same attention to detail. The result is sheet music that is both accurate and enjoyable to play, and remains true to the original performances.

Billy and I are pleased to present the revised sheet music to Piano Man in its entirety.

Enjoy,

David Rosenthal
August 2011

TRAVELIN' PRAYER

Words and Music by
BILLY JOEL

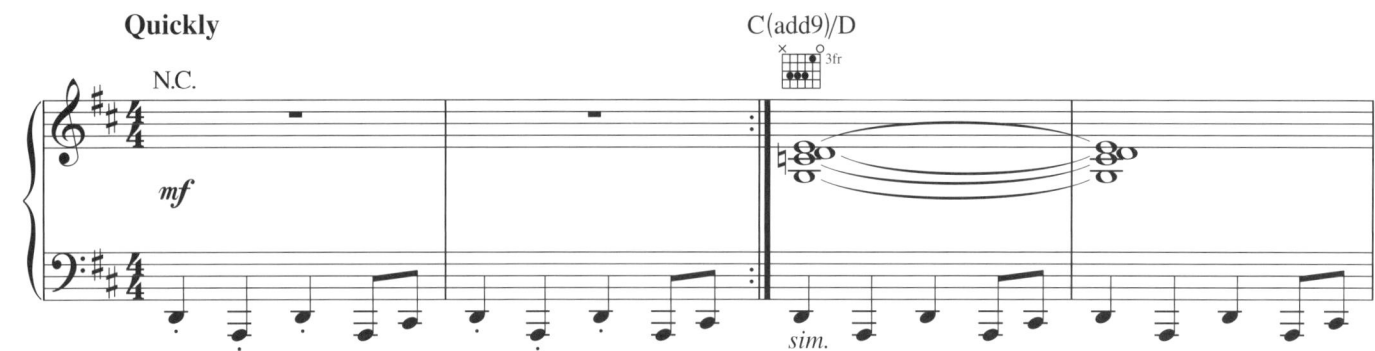
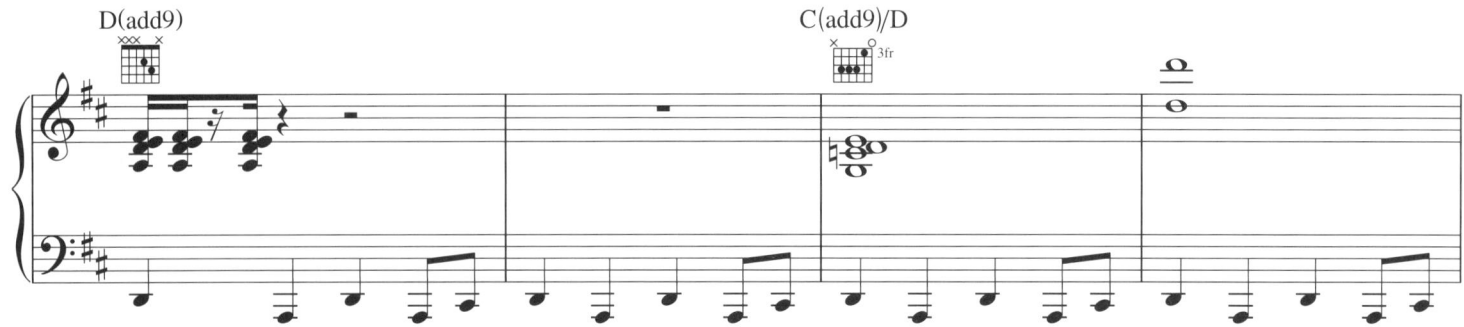
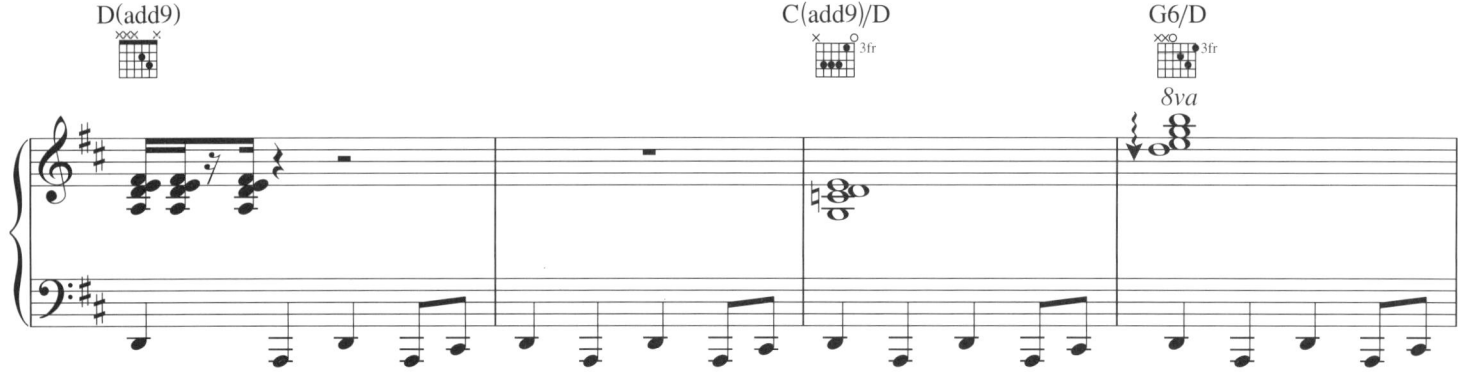
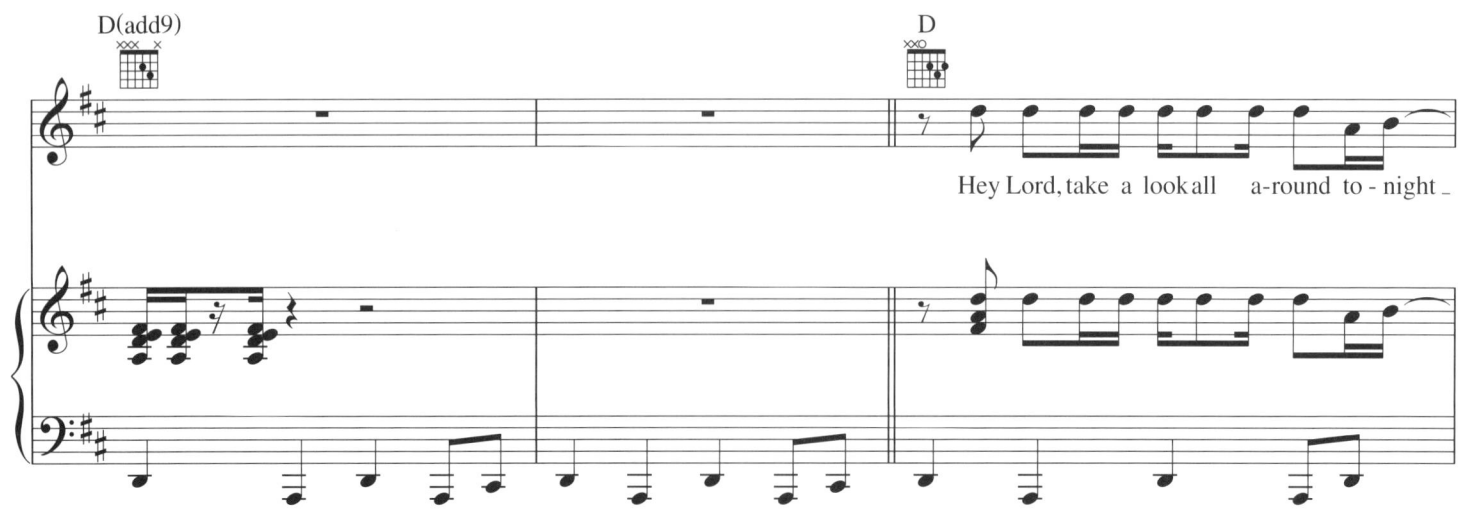

Hey Lord, take a look all a-round to-night___

© 1971, 1974 (Renewed 1999, 2002) IMPULSIVE MUSIC
All Rights Reserved   International Copyright Secured   Used by Permission

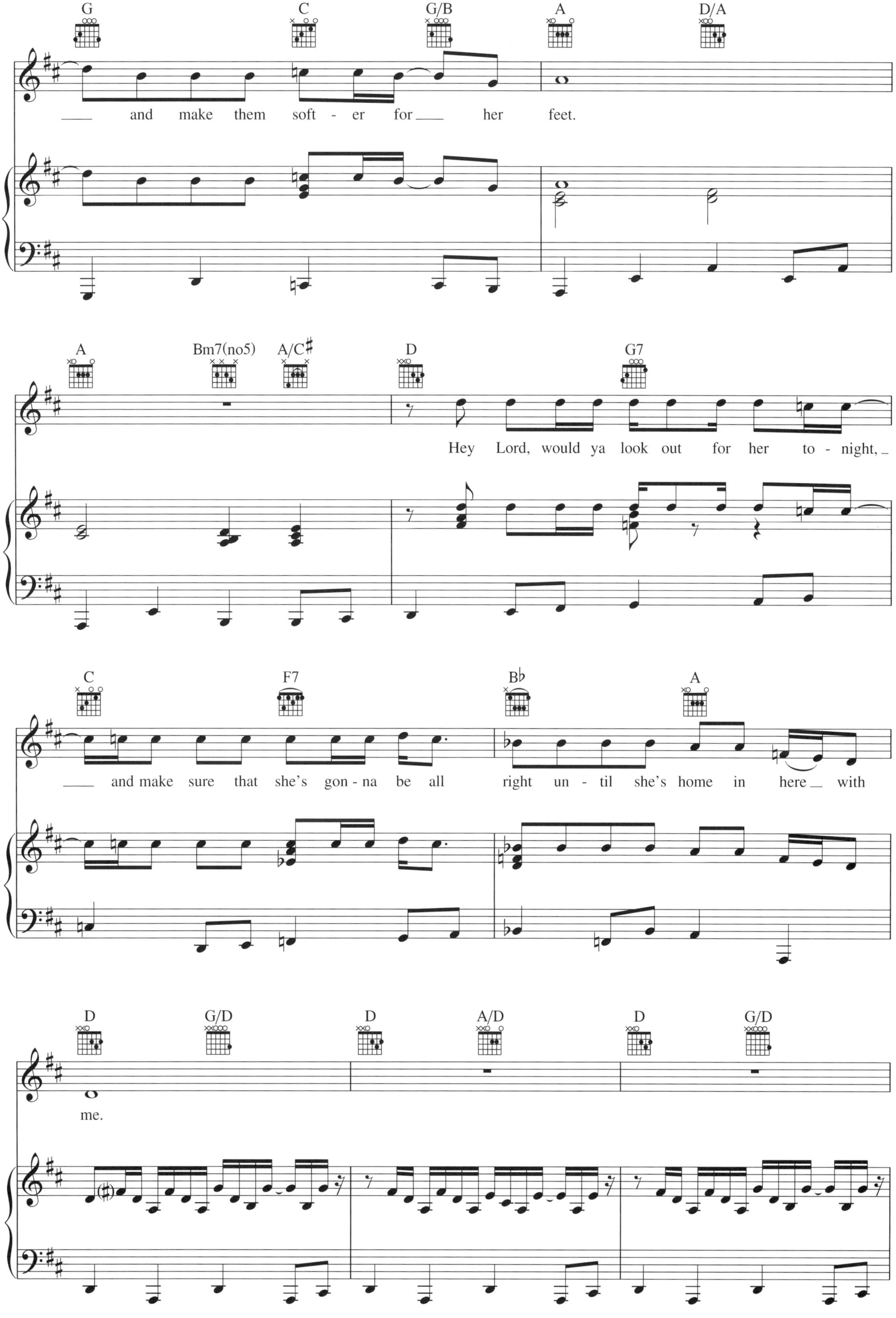
G C G/B A D/A
and make them soft - er for her feet.
A Bm7(no5) A/C♯ D G7
Hey Lord, would ya look out for her to - night,
C F7 B♭ A
and make sure that she's gon - na be all right un - til she's home in here with
D G/D D A/D D G/D
me.

PIANO MAN

Words and Music by
BILLY JOEL

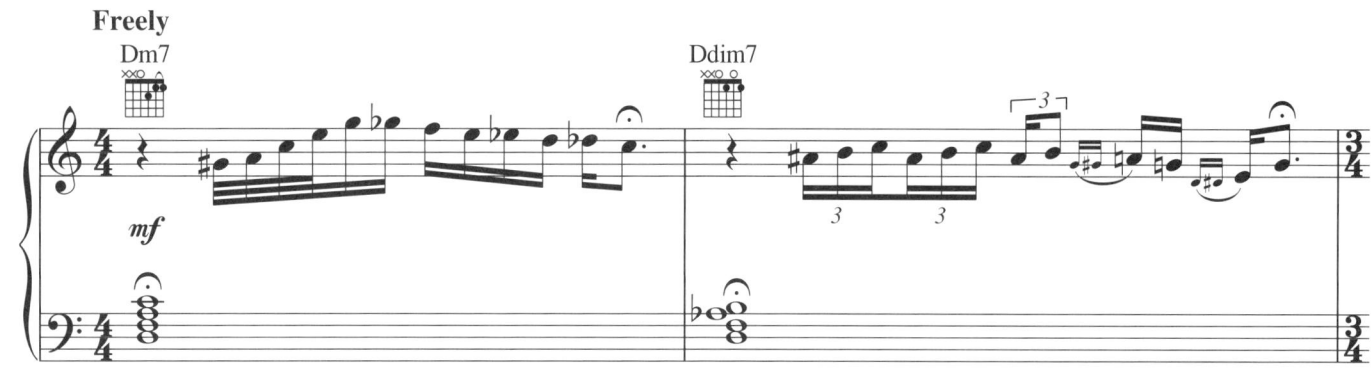
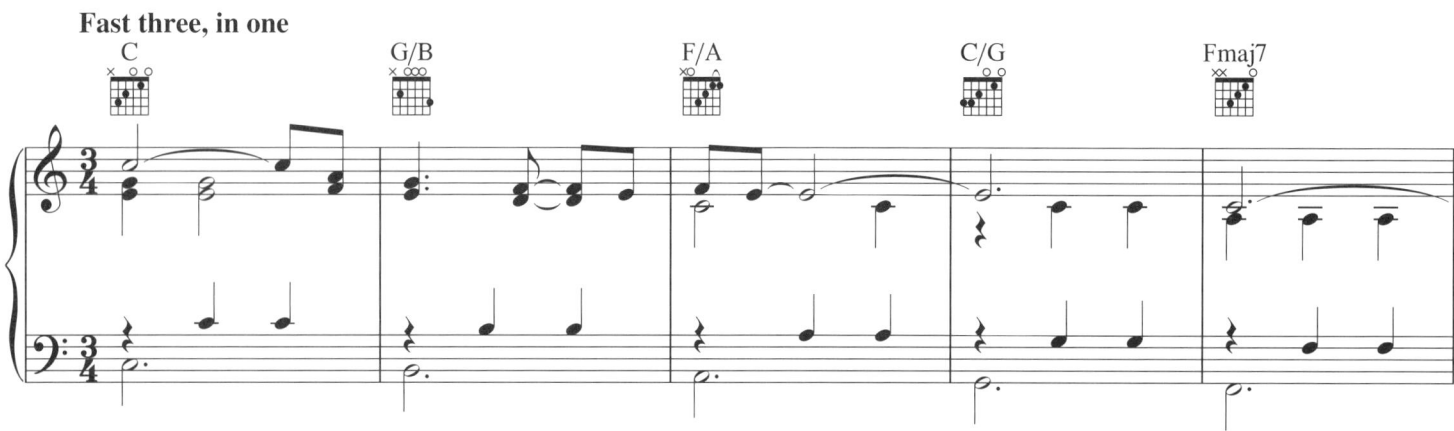
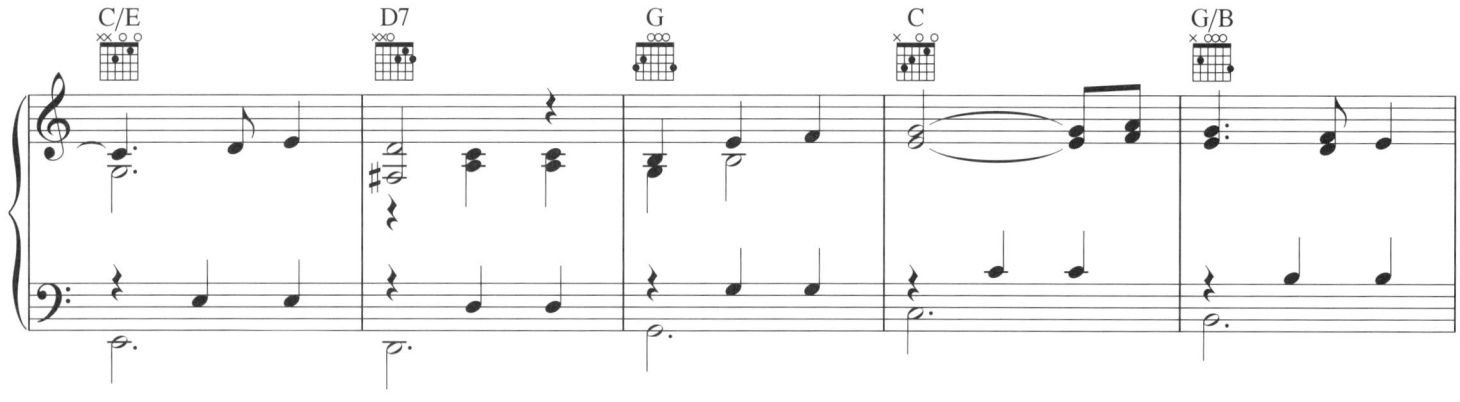
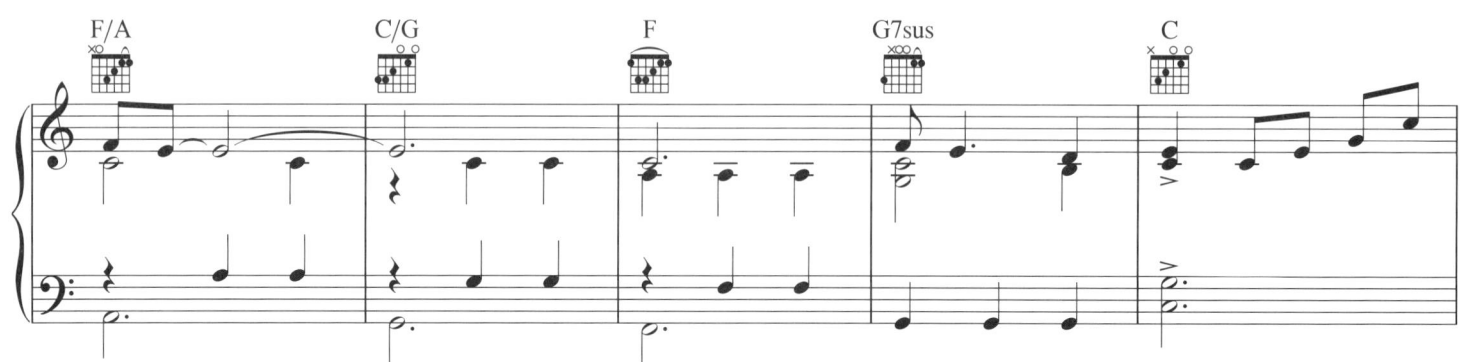

1973, 1974 (Renewed 2001, 2002) JOEL SONGS
All Rights Reserved   International Copyright Secured   Used by Permission

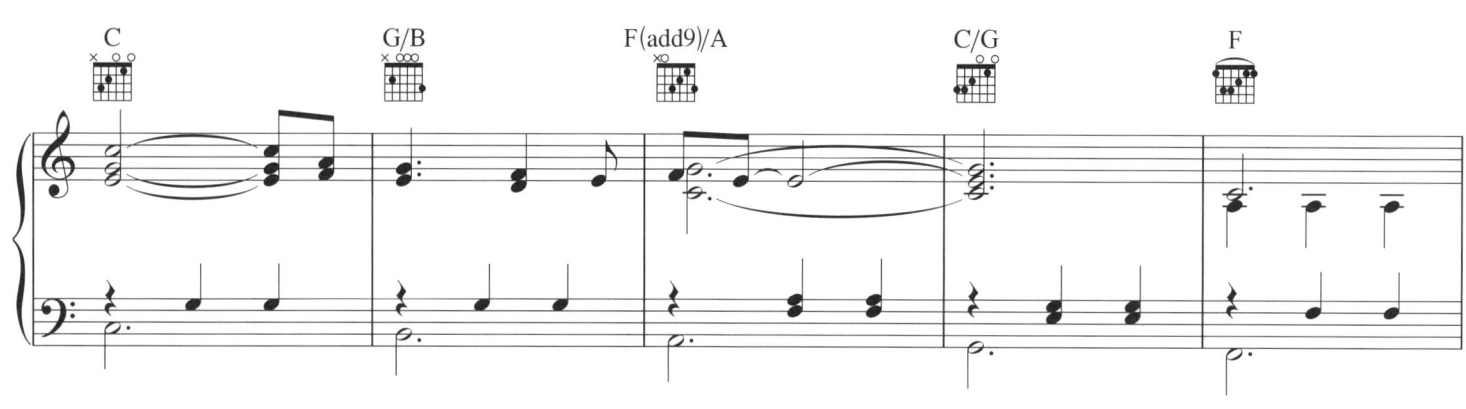
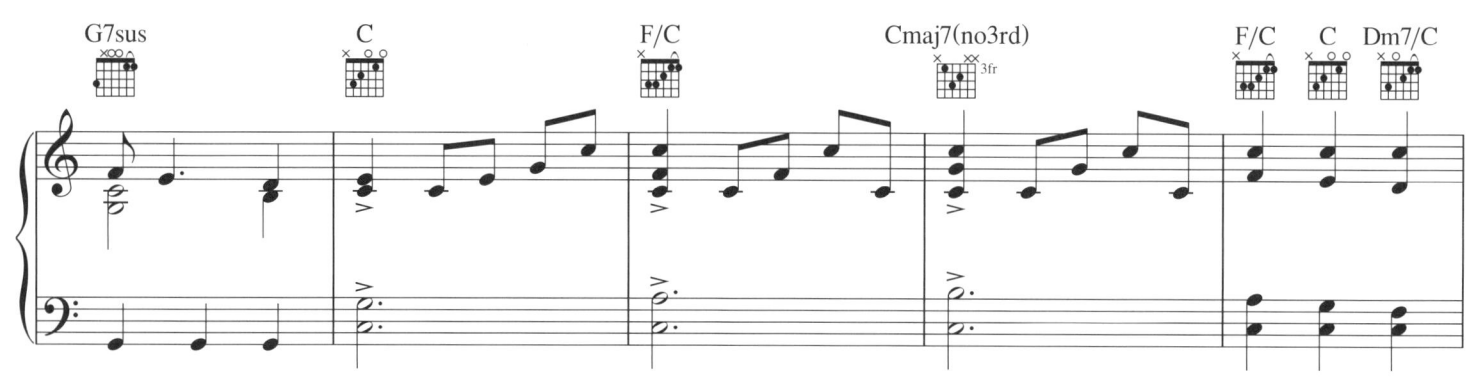
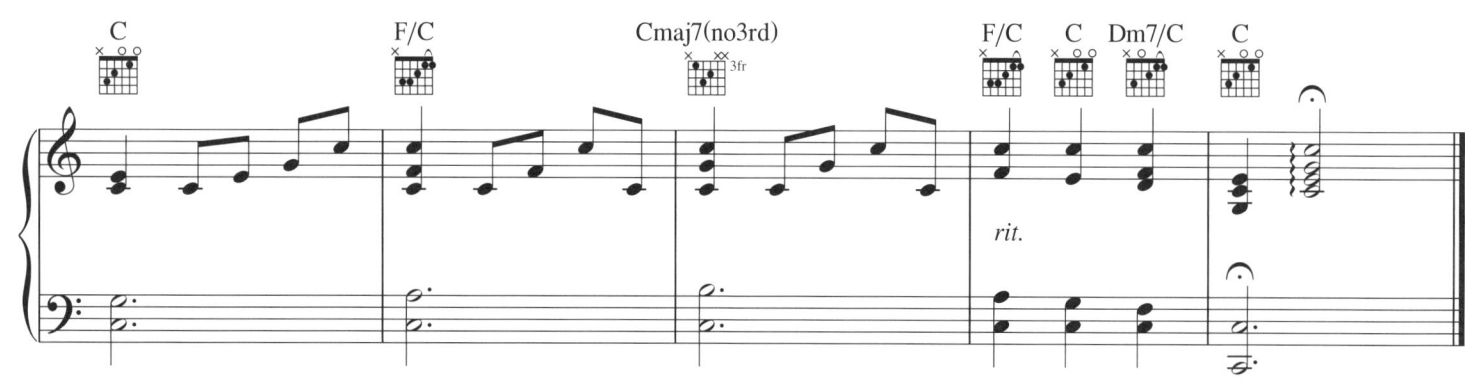

AIN'T NO CRIME

Words and Music by
BILLY JOEL

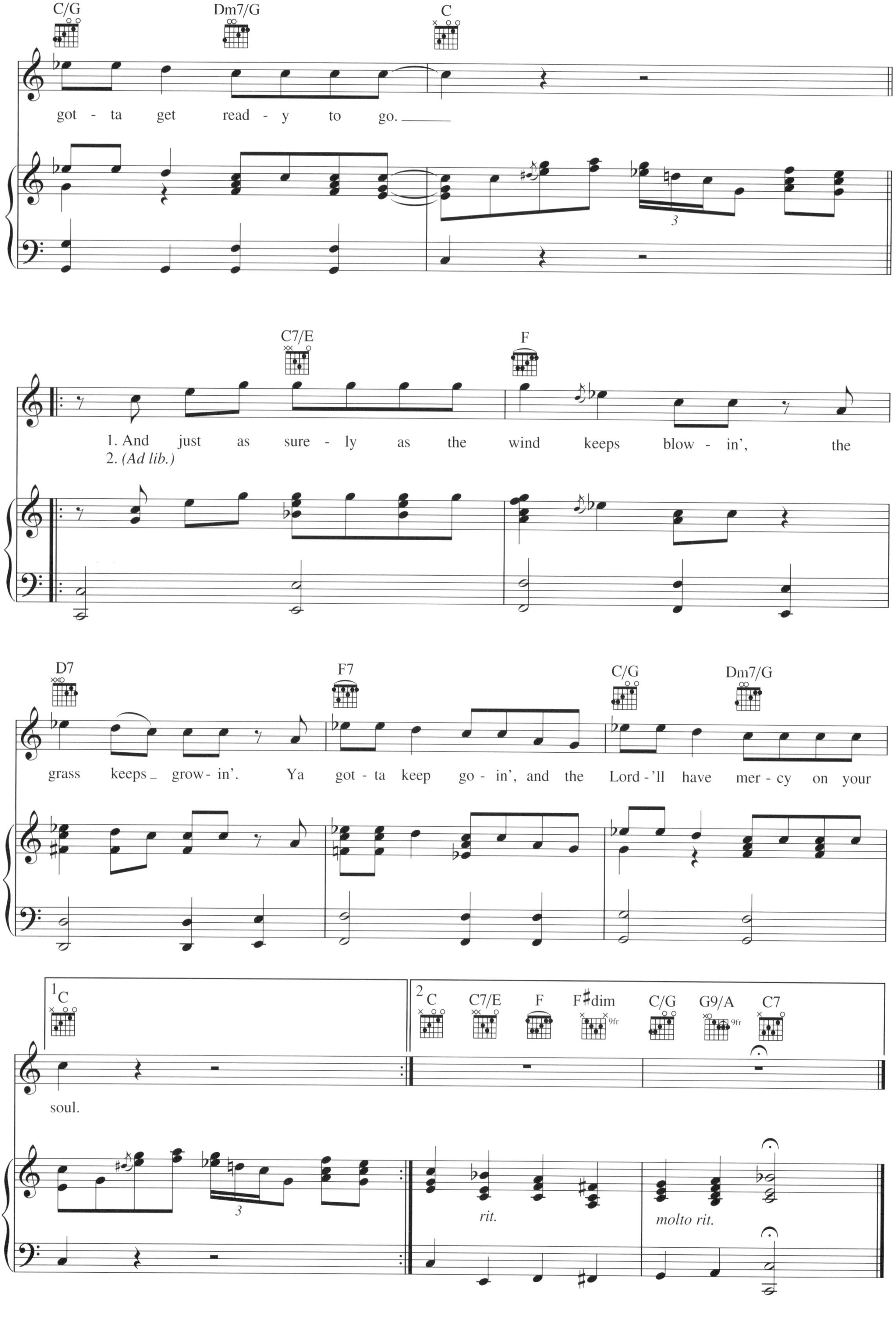
C/G Dm7/G C
got - ta get read - y to go.
C7/E F
1. And just as sure - ly as the wind keeps blow - in', the
2. (Ad lib.)
D7 F7 C/G Dm7/G
grass keeps grow - in'. Ya got - ta keep go - in', and the Lord - 'll have mer - cy on your
1 C
soul.
2 C C7/E F F♯dim C/G G9/A C7
9fr
9fr
rit.
molto rit.

YOU'RE MY HOME

Words and Music by
BILLY JOEL

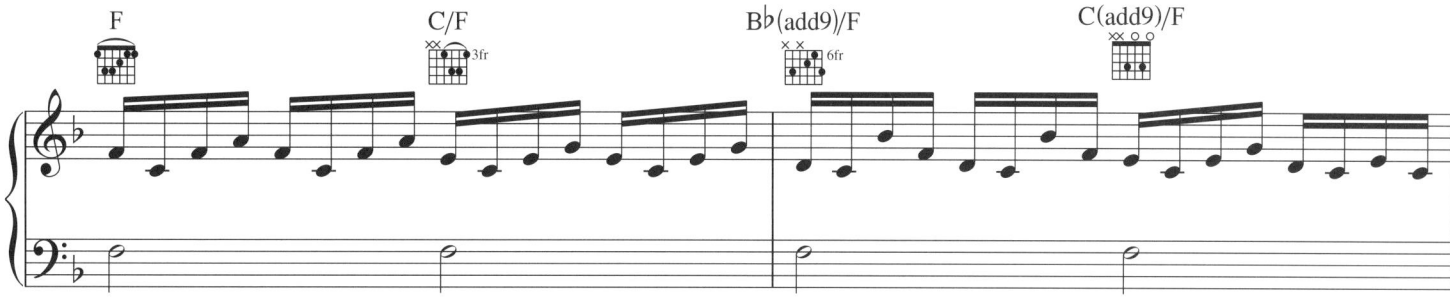
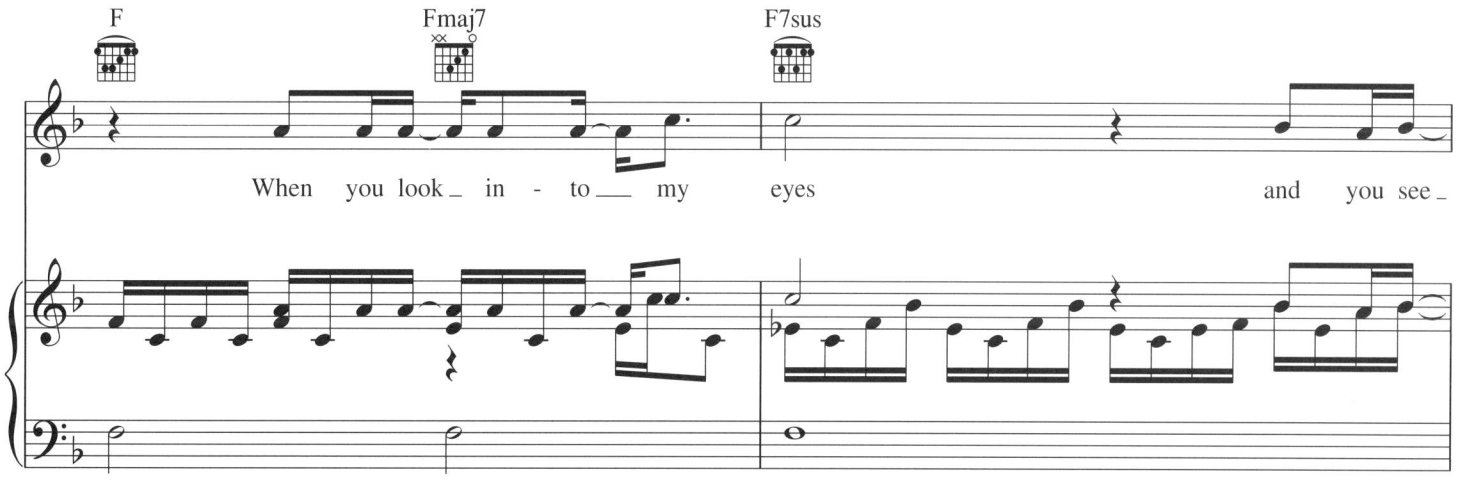
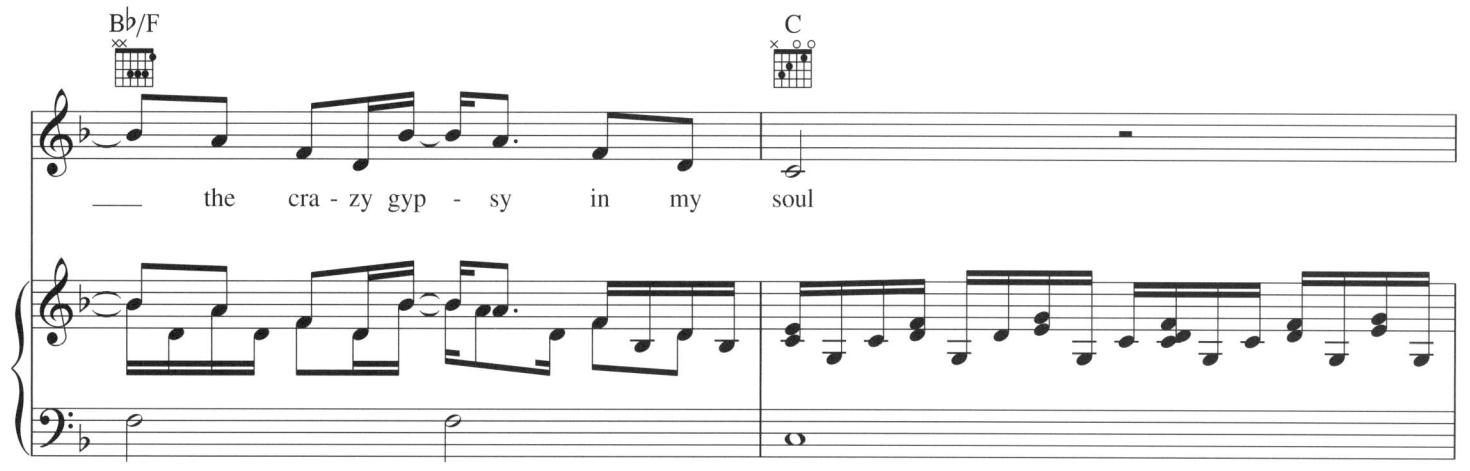

When you look into my eyes and you see the crazy gypsy in my soul

© 1973, 1974 (Renewed 2001, 2002) JOEL SONGS
All Rights Reserved   International Copyright Secured   Used by Permission

(The) BALLAD OF BILLY THE KID

Words and Music by
BILLY JOEL

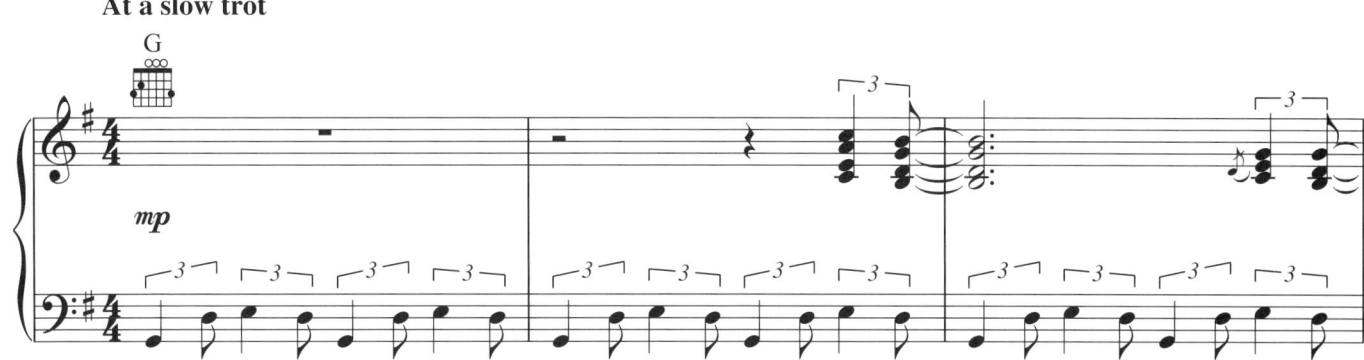

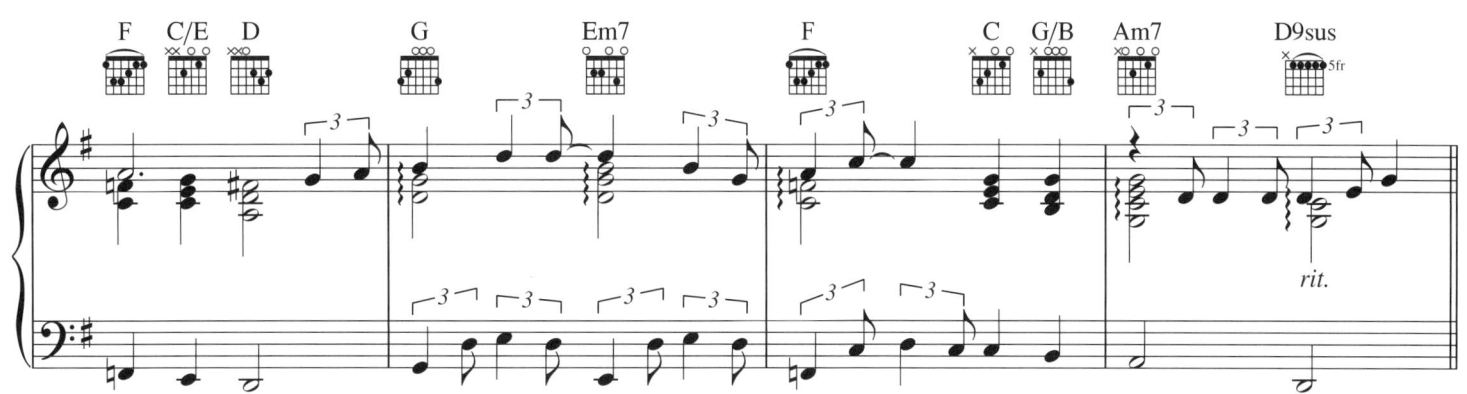

© 1972, 1974 (Renewed 2000, 2002) JOEL SONGS
All Rights Reserved   International Copyright Secured   Used by Permission

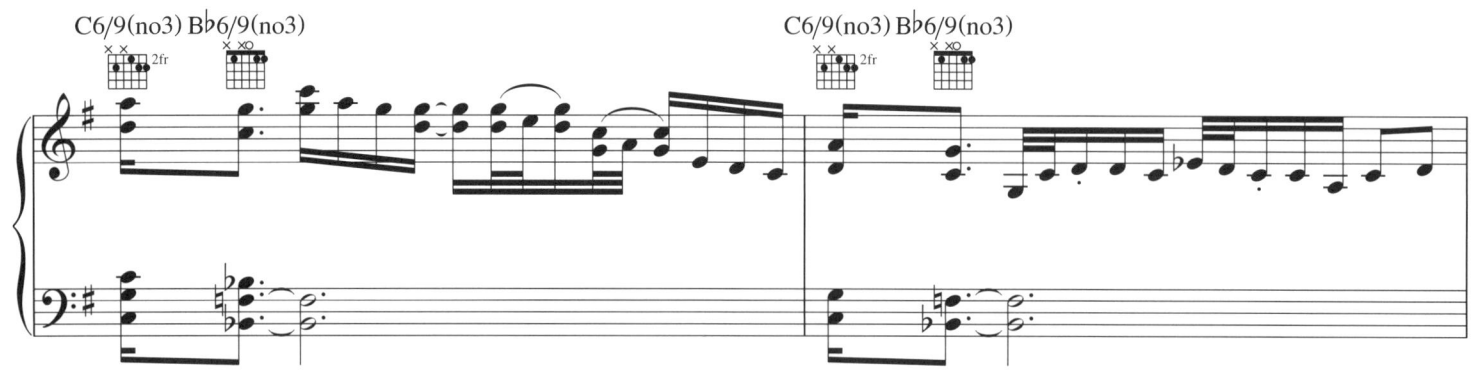
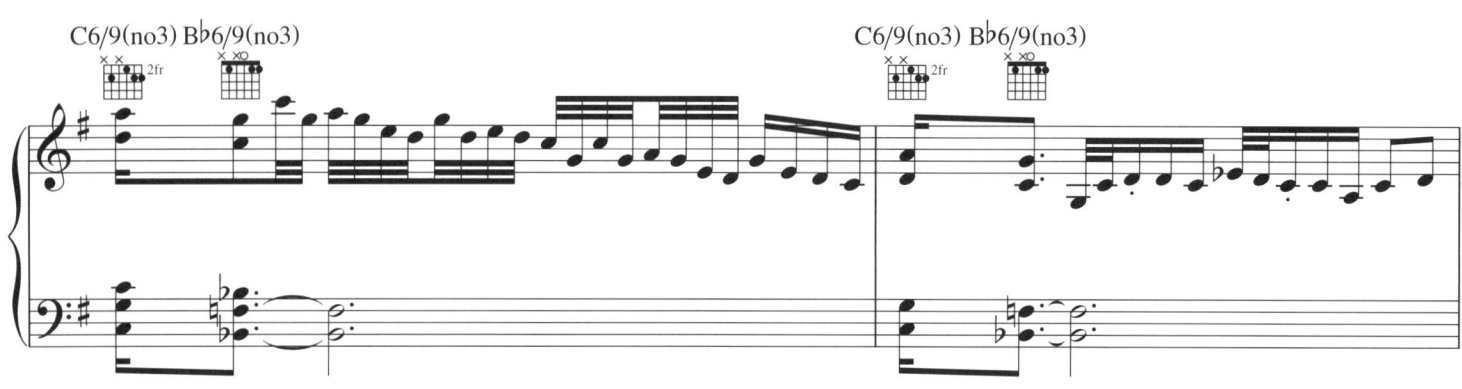
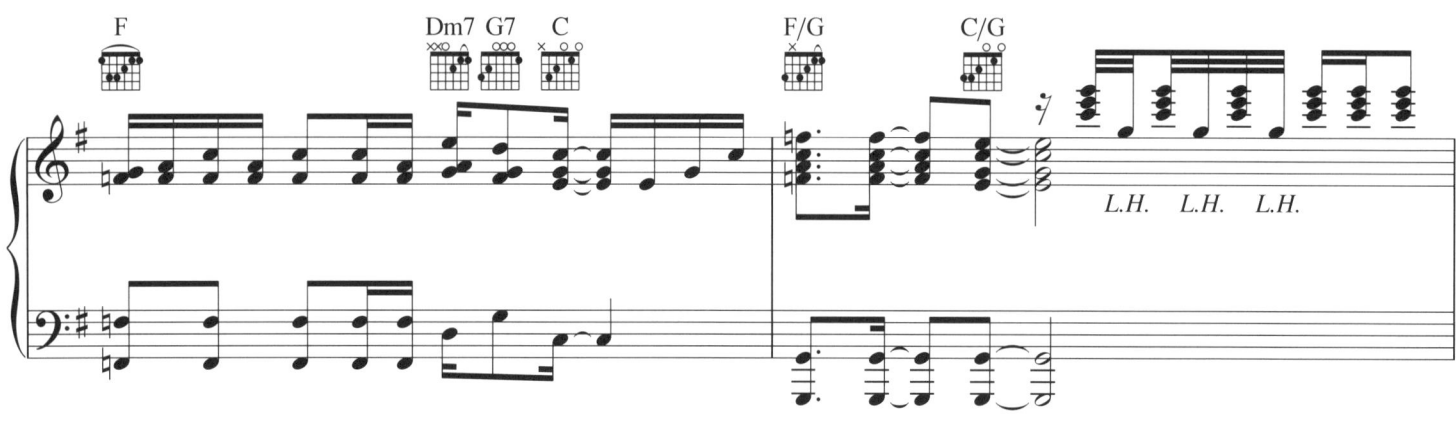
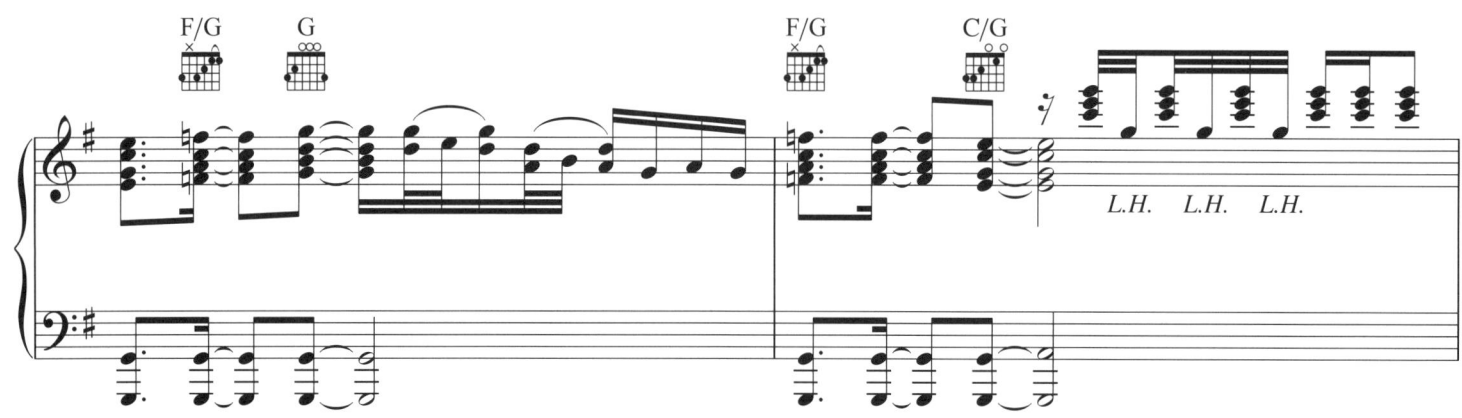

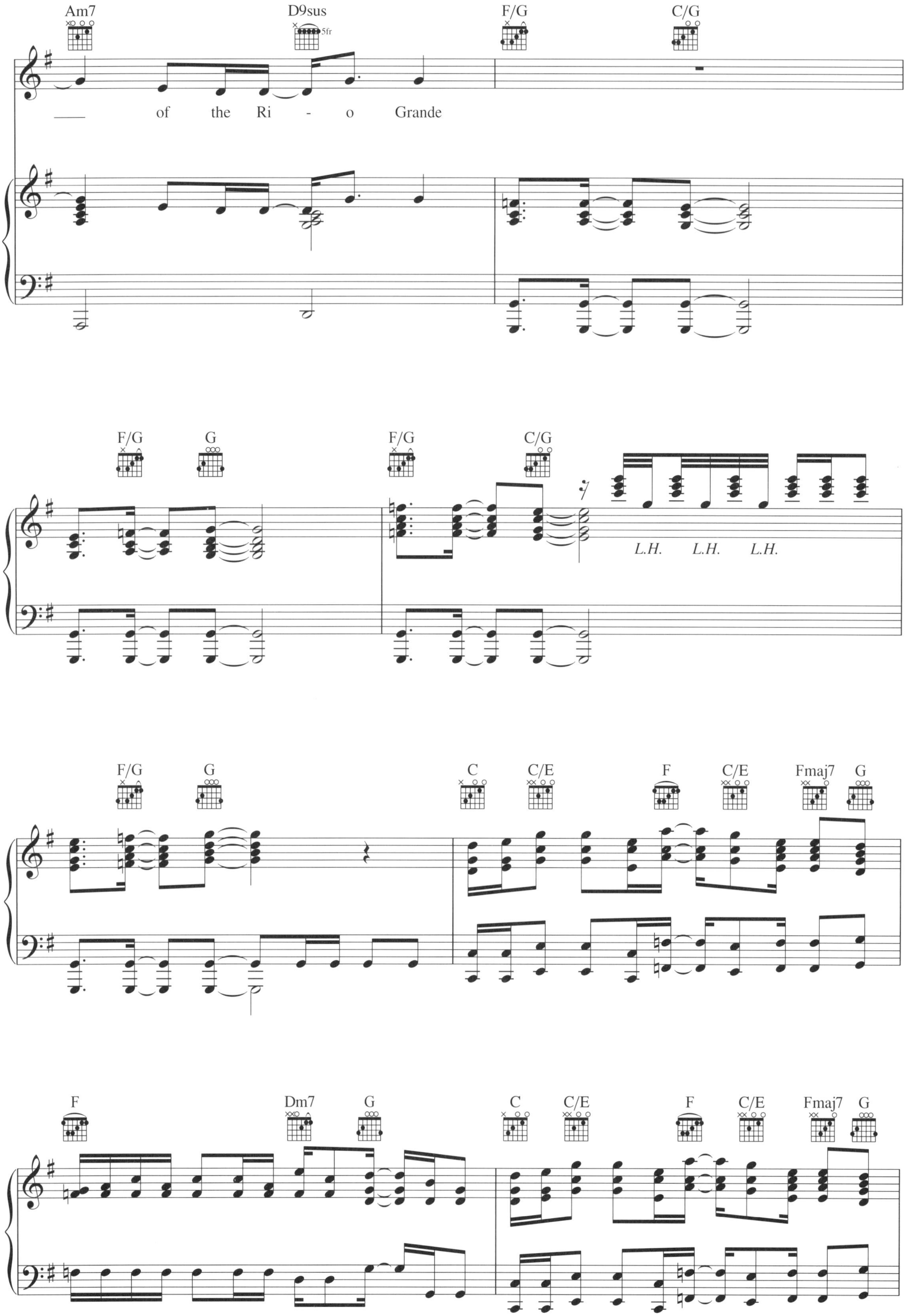
Am7
D9sus
5fr
F/G
C/G
of the Ri - o Grande
F/G
G
F/G
C/G
L.H.
L.H.
L.H.
F/G
G
C
C/E
F
C/E
Fmaj7
G
F
Dm7
G
C
C/E
F
C/E
Fmaj7
G

WORSE COMES TO WORST

Words and Music by
BILLY JOEL

STOP IN NEVADA

Words and Music by
BILLY JOEL

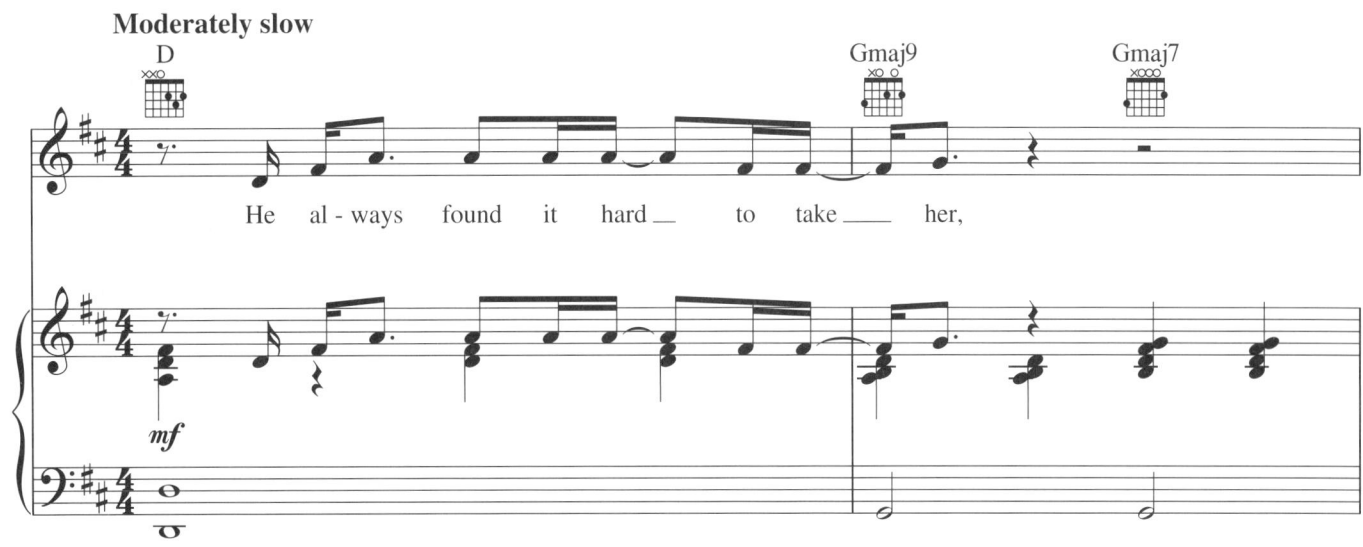

He al-ways found it hard to take her,

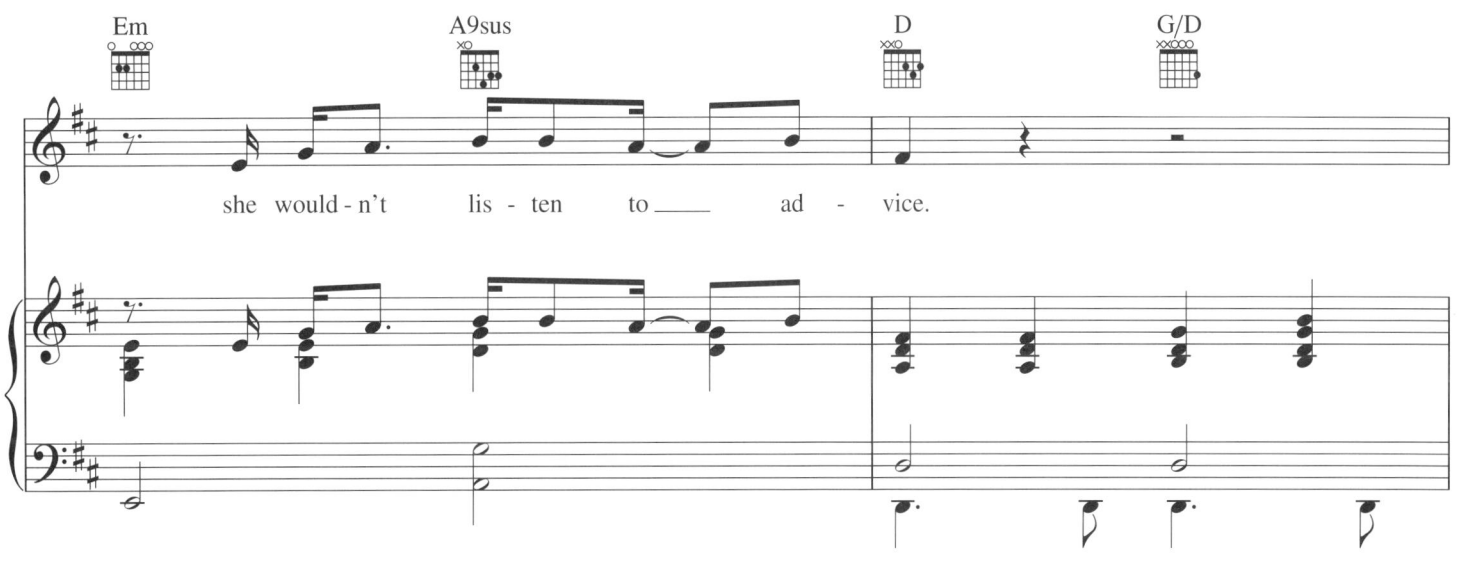

she would-n't lis-ten to ad-vice.

And though he nev-er tried to make her,

© 1973, 1974 (Renewed 2001, 2002) JOEL SONGS
All Rights Reserved   International Copyright Secured   Used by Permission

IF I ONLY HAD THE WORDS
(To Tell You)

Words and Music by
BILLY JOEL

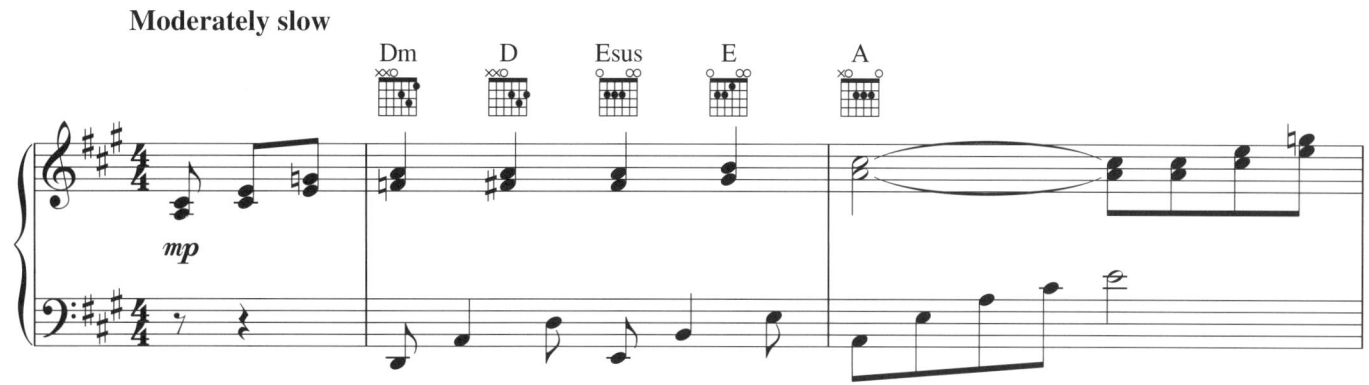

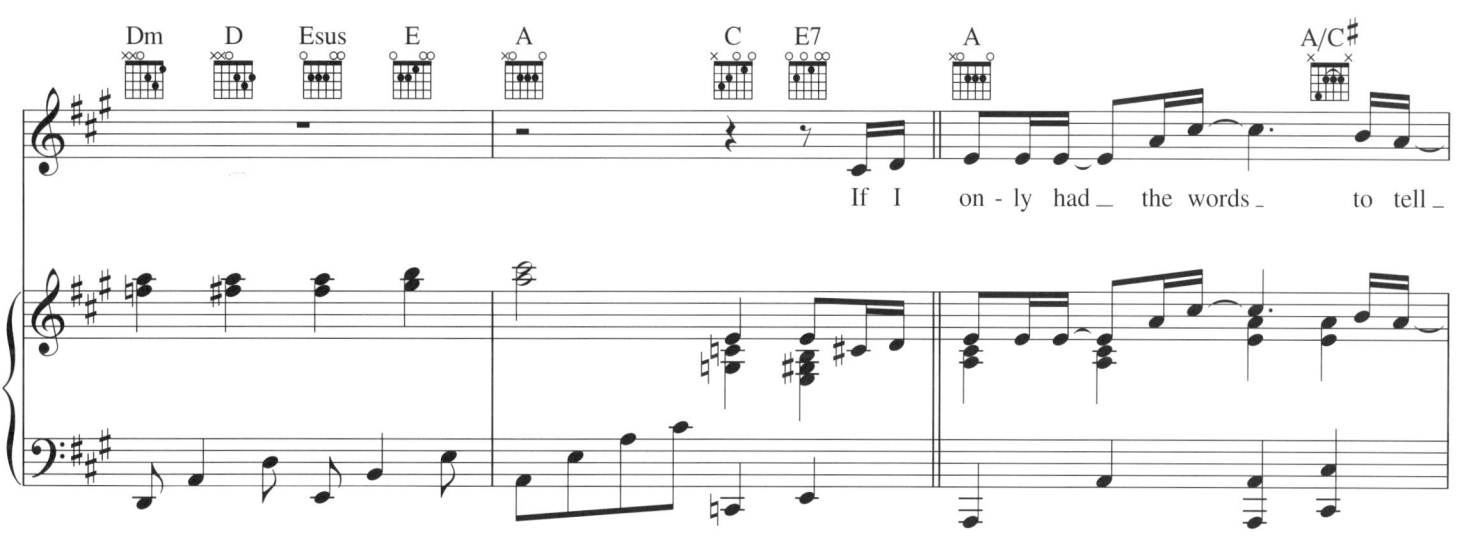

© 1973, 1974 (Renewed 2001, 2002) JOEL SONGS
All Rights Reserved   International Copyright Secured   Used by Permission

SOMEWHERE ALONG THE LINE

Words and Music by
BILLY JOEL

Moderately slow

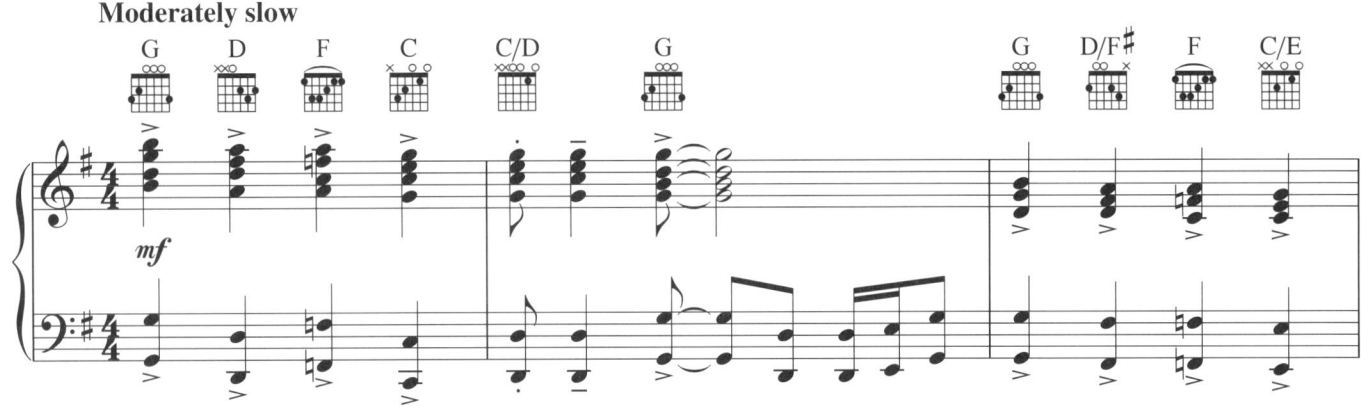

Well, it's a rainy night in Paris, and I'm

sitting by the Seine. It's a pleasure to be soaking in the

© 1973, 1974 (Renewed 2001, 2002) JOEL SONGS
All Rights Reserved   International Copyright Secured   Used by Permission

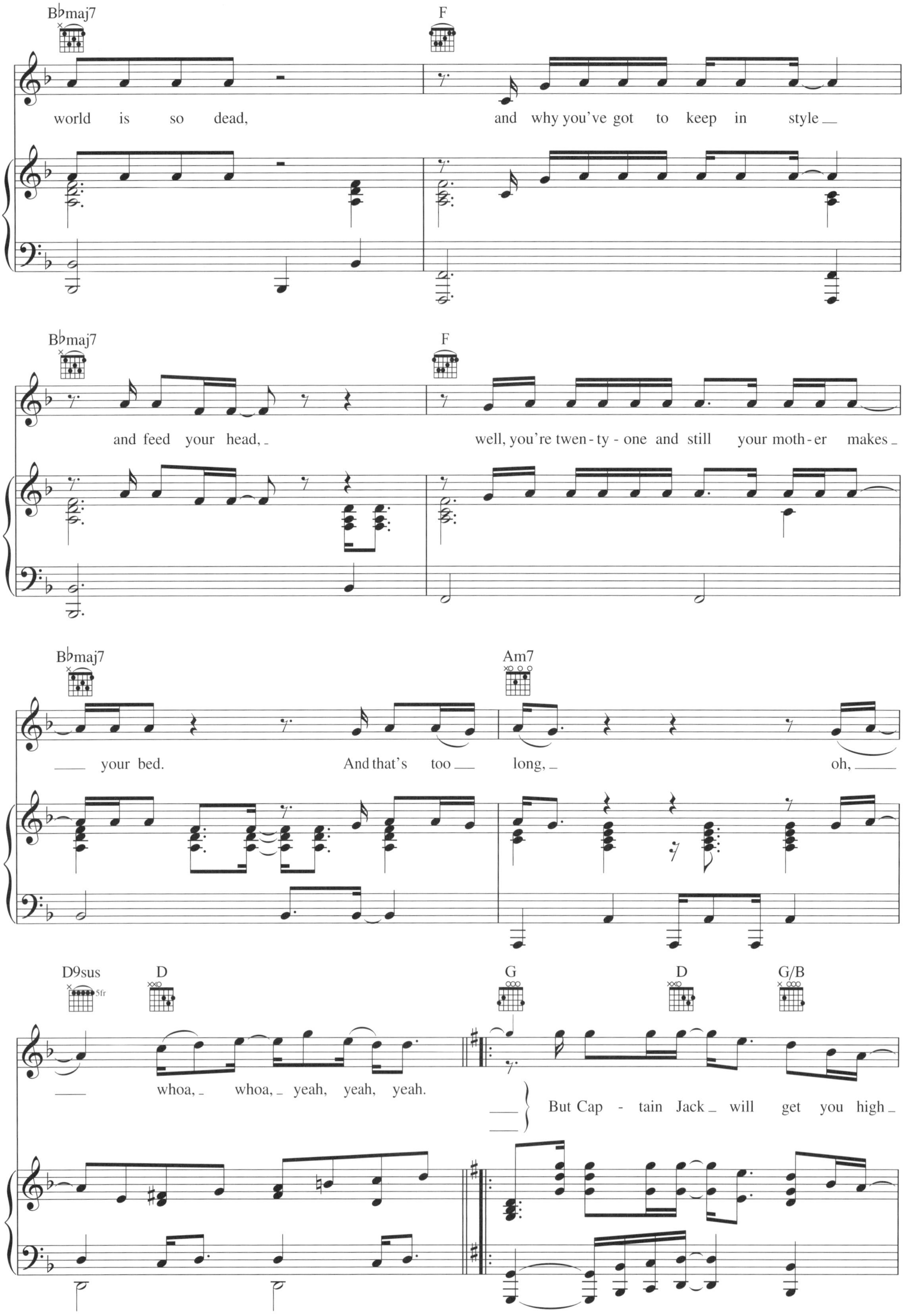
B♭maj7
F
world is so dead,
and why you've got to keep in style
B♭maj7
F
and feed your head,
well, you're twen - ty - one and still your moth - er makes
B♭maj7
Am7
your bed.
And that's too
long,
oh,
D9sus
5fr
D
G
D
G/B
whoa,
whoa,
yeah, yeah, yeah.
But Cap - tain Jack will get you high